Christmas Cookie Cookbook

by Keith Deutsch
illustrated by Robert Mansfield

CINNAMON HOUSE

A Division of Charter Communications, Inc.
A GROSSET AND DUNLAP COMPANY

CHRISTMAS COOKIE COOKBOOK
Copyright © 1978 Grosset & Dunlap, Inc.
All Rights Reserved
A Cinnamon House Edition
ISBN: 0-448-15970-8
Published simultaneously in Canada
Printed in the United States of America

Christmas Cookie Cookbook

Dedicated to Sean McDonald, my first nephew.

Christmas is fun. Cookies are fun. Christmas cookies are double the fun.

THE CHRISTMAS COOKIE COOKBOOK lets you have fun in the kitchen with easy to make cookies of all kinds. Grown-ups will love these cookie recipes too.

Just follow the directions and advice of your Christmas reindeer cookie chef, and you will create perfect cookies every time. All the recipes in this book make delicious cookies for great eating at Christmas time or any time of the year.

Cookies that you make yourself can make your Christmas something special. Here are tasty cookies to give away as presents. Here are cookies to hang on your tree. Here are colorful cookies to decorate gifts for your family and best friends. Here are cookies to stuff stockings for Christmas morning munchies. In THE CHRISTMAS COOKIE COOKBOOK you will find super cookies to nibble the night before Christmas and all winter long. And best of all, you can make them all yourself.

Before you start...
Kitchen tips from your
Christmas cookie chef

Hello kids. Making cookies with me and my elf helper is fun and easy. But before you begin you should always get permission from the grown-ups in your house. Let them help you, especially if you are a beginner in the kitchen.

NEVER use the stove or oven without first getting permission. Be sure the oven is empty. Let your grown-up assistant turn on the oven for you and help you heat up liquids on the top burners. They should also help you do any pouring of hot liquids or syrups. And never use electric mixers without the help of adults.

Cooking is fun, but you have to be careful. You can't be sloppy and make good cookies. Go slowly. Read the recipe carefully.

Make sure that you have all the ingredients before you start. Measure exactly. Make sure you use just the right amount of flour and butter.

Make sure you set the temperature of the oven to the heat called for in the recipe. Let the oven heat up while you measure the ingredients. Don't forget to turn it off when you are finished.

You can't be too careful with hot liquids, pans and hot cookies. You could get burned. Always use dry pot holders to hold hot things. Wet towels or holders don't protect as well as dry pot holders.

You and your adult assistant may want to wear aprons to protect your clothing from spills and splashes. Boys should not feel uncomfortable wearing aprons. Great male chefs wear them all the time.

Always wash your hands before you begin on any recipe. And always clean up after yourself so the kitchen is as nice to work in as you found it.

Snicker Doodles

Here are cinnamony delicious cookies from
Pennsylvania Dutch Christmas cookie kitchens.
These have been made for over a hundred years in
Pennsylvania!

Here's what you need

½ cup butter
¾ cup granulated sugar
1 egg
1¼ cups flour
¼ teaspoon salt
½ teaspoon baking soda
1 teaspoon cream of
   tartar

Later you will also need
   1 tablespoon
   granulated sugar and
   1 tablespoon
   cinnamon.

Tools

Measuring spoons
Measuring Cups
Cooking spoon
Large mixing bowl
Cup
Flour sifter
Wax paper
Large plate
Small plate
Cookie sheet (ungreased)
Spatula
Cookie cooling rack

Here's what you do

1   Measure butter and measure sugar. Put them in
the large bowl.

2   Push the sugar into the butter with the back of a
spoon and mix them together. If you let the butter sit
until soft it is easier to do this. Mix and push until the
butter and sugar are a smooth paste.

3   Break the egg into the cup. Be sure to remove any
bits of shell that might have fallen into the cup. Drop
the egg from the cup into the bowl.

4   Beat the mixture with a spoon until
VERY well mixed.

5   Measure the flour, the salt, the baking soda and the
cream of tartar over wax paper into the sifter. Sift
the mixture over wax paper.

6 Take the wax paper with the mixed flour and dump about half of it into the large bowl with the egg mixture. Stir slowly with a mixing spoon.

7 Add the rest of the sifted flour to the egg mixture and stir slowly again. You will have a sticky, light yellow dough. Cover the mixing bowl with a plate and put in the refrigerator for one hour.

8 The dough should get cold and hard. After the dough has been refrigerated, set the oven to 400 degrees.

9 Mix the tablespoons of sugar and cinnamon in a small plate.

10 Be sure your hands are clean. Break off a bit of cold dough and roll it into a ball. It should be about the size of a walnut or slightly larger.

11 Roll the ball in the cinnamon and sugar dish. Put it on the cookie sheet. Make more balls the same way and place on the sheet. Leave plenty of room between balls.

12 When the cookie sheet is full, place it carefully in the oven with the aid of your adult assistant. Use pot holders.

13 Don't open the oven for at least 10 minutes. When you do, the Snicker Doodles will have flattened out into crinkly cookies. If the edges are not brown, bake them another minute or two.

14 Take the sheet out of the oven with pot holders and the help of your adult assistant. Remove the cookies with a spatula to a cooling rack. Be careful. The Snicker Doodles are soft until they cool.

There are no variations to this recipe. You'll make great cookies every time.

When you mix butter with other ingredients into a smooth paste, cooks call this "creaming the butter." To cream butter or other soft shortening, you push the sugar or dry material into the butter with the back of a spoon. At first the butter will stick to the spoon. Push it off and keep on mixing. Push and mix and the butter and sugar will smooth out into a creamy paste. NEVER heat butter to help make it soft for creaming. Let butter stand and it will get soft for mixing with other ingredients.

Always keep a few towels handy. And a wet sponge for cleaning up spills and drips right when they happen. Watch the floor and be sure nothing is left there. A slip on a wet floor when cooking is very dangerous.

Always help your adult assistant clean up. Wash the dishes and return all ingredients and tools to their places.

Caramel Cookie Bars

Here's a recipe for nutty-sweet squares that crunch when you chew them. Perfect for a night before Christmas snack. They're almost candy.

Here's what you need

¼ cup of butter
1 cup dark brown sugar, packed
1 egg
2 teaspoons vanilla extract
½ cup flour
1 teaspoon baking powder
½ teaspoon salt
1 cup chopped walnuts or pecans (8 ounces)

Tools

Measuring cups
Measuring spoons
Cooking spoon (long handled)
Saucepan
Greased cookie pan (8 by 8 by 2 inches)
Cookie rack
Small knife
Pot holders

Here's what you do

1   Put butter in the saucepan over very low heat until it is just melted.

2   Add brown sugar and stir constantly until it melts too. This should not take very long. Remember to use very low heat.

3   Remove the saucepan from the heat and let it cool. Measure all other ingredients while butter and brown sugar cool.

4   Add the egg to the saucepan and add the vanilla extract. Beat the mixture with a spoon until well mixed.

5   Add flour, baking powder and salt. Mix well. Turn oven on to 350 degrees.

6 Pour the thick mixture into the greased pan. Spoon it out if necessary.

7 Sprinkle the surface with nuts.

8 Use pot holders and put pan in hot oven. Bake for 25 minutes.

9 Take caramel cake out of oven with pot holders and cool the pan on a cookie rack. In ten minutes or so you can cut the cake into caramel bars with the knife.

These cookies store best in tightly covered containers. They will be fudgy. They are best if not dried out.

Helpful hint

Break your egg over a cup by tapping sharply on the rim. Pour egg into the saucepan from the cup. One sharp tap will crack the shell. If you hold the egg in two hands it will open nicely and the liquid will slip right out. Be sure to check that no pieces of the shell fall into the cup.

Chocolate Chip Christmas Brownies

Yes, these are brownies and not cookies. But what dee-licious and chocolate rich brownies these are. You don't mind that they're not cookies, do you?

Here's what you need

¾ cup flour
½ teaspoon baking powder
   (double-acting)
½ teaspoon salt
1 cup granulated sugar
½ cup vegetable oil
2 eggs
1 teaspoon vanilla extract
2 envelopes unsweetened,
   pre-melted chocolate
4 ounces or ¾ cup chopped or
   whole walnuts
6 ounces of semi-sweet
   chocolate bits (chips)

Tools

Measuring spoons
Measuring cups
Pot holders
Cooking spoon
8 by 8 by 2 inch
   baking pan
Large mixing bowl
Flour sifter
Cup
Rubber scraper or
   spatula
Wire rack
Knife
Wax paper

Here's what you do

1 Set oven to 350 degrees.

2 Grease the baking pan with a small piece of butter held in a paper towel.

3 Measure the flour, the salt and the baking powder into the sifter. Sift over the wax paper. Then drop into large mixing bowl.

4 Measure the sugar and add to the flour in the bowl. Mix.

5 Pour the half cup of vegetable oil into center of bowl. Do not mix.

6 Break the two eggs into the cup. Pour eggs into mixing bowl. Do not stir.

7 Add the vanilla extract. Add the pre-melted chocolate. Now you can stir. Stir slowly. Then mix quickly. Keep mixing until you have a smooth, deep brown batter.

8 Add most of the nuts, but not all. If they seem too large, break them into smaller bits in your fingers.

9 Add the semi-sweet chocolate chips. Stir until the chips and nuts are well mixed in the batter.

10 Use a rubber scraper or spatula to pour the batter into the greased baking pan. Get all the batter off the sides of the mixing bowl. Push the batter into the corners of the baking pan.

11 Put the pan in the oven using pot holders. Let it bake for 30 to 35 minutes. The cake will rise and the top will look bumpy. The sides will be crisp and away from the pan.

12 Take pan from oven and rest on wire rack to cool 20 minutes. Cut into brownies.

Variations are limitless. You can use peanuts or any nuts you like instead of walnuts. You can add butterscotch chips instead of chocolate bits. You can even add raisins to the batter.

A word about mixing, stirring, and beating. Beating
means to move your spoon around fast to blend
ingredients very QUICKLY. Mixtures with eggs are
often beaten. There are rotary hand beaters which are
fun to use which will do this job quickly. But a good
spoon works just as well.

Stirring means SLOWLY moving your spoon inside a
bowl or saucepan to mix the ingredients.
Mixing is in between beating and stirring. You can use a
spoon (my favorite) or if the mixture is very thick, use a
fork. Mix ingredients well with steady strokes.
But do not over mix.

If you make a lot of crisp cookies and they become
soggy or soft after a time, you can revive them. Heat
them in the oven at about 325 degrees for about five
minutes. They'll come out crisp and fresh as ever.
Soft cookies that dry out and become hard are not stale.
You can revive them easily by adding a slice of raw
apple to the cookie jar. Change the apple slice every
day. The cookies will become soft again in a day or two.

Orange Marmalade Tart Cookies

Very orangey cookies that don't taste like anything else you've ever munched. Sweet and tart and great with milk.

Here's what you need

⅔ cup of sugar
½ cup softened butter
1 egg
6 tablespoons orange marmalade (Imported kind with thick orange pieces is the best)
1½ cups of sifted flour
1¼ teaspoons baking powder
optional: rind of fresh orange coarsely grated.

Tools

Measuring spoons
Measuring cups
Cooking spoon
Cookie sheets lightly greased
Wire rack
Wax paper
Mixing bowl
Teaspoon
optional: coarse grater

Here's what you do

1 Heat oven to 375 degrees. Take out butter and let it get soft. Arrange other tools and ingredients.

2 Measure soft butter in measuring cup and drop into mixing bowl.

3 Measure sugar in measuring cup and drop in bowl with butter. Beat sugar and butter with cooking spoon, mashing it around until it blends well. It will become fluffy.

4 Optional: Have your adult assistant help you with the grater and grate the orange peel over the butter and sugar blend into the bowl.

5 Sift flour over wax paper or if you are using the recommended pre-sifted "instant" flour, you can just measure 2½ cups and drop it in the mixing bowl. If not, take sifted flour on wax paper and slide it into mixing bowl.

6 Add marmalade and baking powder to mixing bowl. Mix up the dough well until everything is blended through and through.

7 Take big round teaspoonfuls of the dough and slide each one down on the lightly greased cookie sheet. Each teaspoonful of dough will make a cookie.

8 Bake cookies about 8 minutes until the edges get brown. Remove from baking sheet and cool on the wire rack. Store in tightly covered containers.

Helpful hint

Let cookie sheets cool before using them again in between batches of baking. Don't wash cookie sheets in between baking batches. Just wipe them clean with a paper towel.

Candy Cane Cookies

These are light and crunchy peppermint meringues that are fun to make and eat. They are made without flour and melt in your mouth. Great with ice cream.

Here's what you need

A few candy canes
4 egg whites
¼ teaspoon cream of tartar
¼ teaspoon salt
1 cup sugar
1 teaspoon peppermint
   extract

Tools

Measuring cup
Measuring spoons
Baking sheets rubbed with
   butter or margarine
Rotary hand beater
Tablespoon
Small mixing bowl

Here's what you do

1 Heat oven to 275 degrees. Meringues are made of egg whites and sugar that are dried crispy in a slow cooking oven. You don't use too much heat. You let the cookies bake a long time instead.

2 Have your grown-up assistant help you remove the yolks from the four eggs. To do this, you crack open the egg over a bowl and hold the liquid in between the open shell. The white will slip out, but if you are careful, the yolk will stay inside the shell. Practice. It is not an easy trick. Put the egg whites and peppermint extract in a bowl.

3   Once you have four egg whites in the mixing bowl, add the cream of tartar and salt and beat with the rotary beater or with a spoon or fork until the egg white thickens. It will start to make sharp points as it thickens.

4   Add sugar one tablespoon at a time and continue beating the mixture. When it is very stiff and shiny it is ready.

5   Take a tablespoon of the meringue dough and drop it on a cookie sheet that has been rubbed with some butter or margarine. Use just enough to make the surface greasy.

6   Keep adding tablespoon globs of the meringue dough to the cookie sheet until the sheet is filled with white mounds.

7 Take a candy cane and crush it under the bottom of a measuring cup. Dust the candy cane bits on the meringue mounds.

8 You may have to use more than one cookie sheet to use up all the meringue dough. When the dough is finished, put the cookie sheets in the oven and bake for one hour. When an hour is up, the cookies should be firm and white, but not browned. Turn off the oven and let the cookies cool inside the oven for about another hour. Store in a tightly covered container.

For variety, you can add food coloring to parts of the dough after separating it into separate bowls. Then you can have red, white, and green meringues.

Helpful hint

Always grease your cookie sheet very lightly. Too much butter will make your cookies run and lose their shape when cooking.

Oatmeal Butter Bars

Tasty, toffee sweet cookies that fill you up with nutty oatmeal flavor. Good in the morning before you go out to build a snowman.

Here's what you need

1 cup DARK brown sugar
1/2 teaspoon salt
1/2 cup of butter
1 teaspoon baking powder
2 cups quick-cooking oatmeal (uncooked)

Tools

Measuring spoons
Measuring cups
Cooking spoon (long handled)
Baking pan (8 by 8 by 2 inches)
Saucepan
Pot holders
Cookie cooling rack
Small knife

Here's what you do

1 Measure sugar and butter. Combine them in a saucepan. With the aid of your adult assistant put saucepan over VERY LOW heat on top of the stove. Stir with spoon until butter melts.

2 Remove from heat. Turn oven on to 350 degrees. Grease baking pan with a bit of butter.

3 Add salt, baking powder and oatmeal to the saucepan. Stir until well mixed.

4 Using pot holders, pour cookie mixture into the greased pan.

5 Bake in oven for about 25 minutes. The edges of the cookie mixture will be brown. The center will be bubbly.

6 Remove from oven with pot holders and place on cookie rack to cool. Cut into bars when cool about ten minutes later.

These cookies store best in tightly covered containers.

VARIATIONS: Sprinkle raisins or chopped nuts over the mixture in pan before baking.

Baking is as important as making. This means that putting the ingredients together carefully is only half the job of a good cookie chef.

You have to set the oven to the right temperature *(only with the permission and help of your adult assistant, of course)* and you have to keep the cookies in the oven the right time.

But not all ovens work the same. Some run cooler or hotter than the temperature set on their controls. One way to be sure the oven works right is to check its temperature with an oven thermometer.

Don't open the oven more than once or twice during the given cooking time. This reduces the temperature and could add baking time. Be sure to close the oven door tightly and gently. After the given time is over, however, open the oven door every minute or so to see how your cookies are doing.

Most cookies are done when brown around the edges. Bar cookies made in a single cake in a pan are done when a tooth pick slipped into their center comes out without any dough sticking to it.

Christmas Chocolate Macaroons

These are small cookies, very chocolatey and chewy. One is not enough. You can't stop eating them.

Here's what you need

2 eggs
1 cup fine, granulated sugar
2½ cups ground almonds
1½ ounces (squares) bitter chocolate (grated or chopped up)

Tools

Measuring spoons
Measuring cups
Cookie sheet (greased with a bit of butter)

Mixing bowl
Grater (optional)
Knife

Here's what you do

1 Mix eggs and sugar in bowl until they become thick and almost white.

2 Grate the chocolate or scrape it into thin pieces with the knife and chop it. Perhaps your adult assistant can grate the chocolate for you.

3 If you buy ground almonds just add them to the grated chocolate. If you buy unground or chopped or slivered almonds, buy them with their skins on for extra flavor. You can buy them ground, or grind them yourself by wrapping them in a cloth napkin and pounding them with a hammer or rolling pin. Best is to buy ground almonds.

4 Mix almond and chocolate mixture into the bowl with the eggs and sugar. Mix well.

5 Turn on oven to 400 degrees.

6 Drop the dough by teaspoonfuls onto the cookie sheet. Remember to grease the sheet. Leave about 2 inches between each cookie.

7 Put in the oven using pot holders and have your adult assistant help you.

8 Bake for about three minutes.

9 Reduce heat to 350 degrees. Bake for about 10 minutes more.

10 Cookies are done when they hold their shape and when a toothpick inserted in their middle comes out clean.

11 Remove cookies from oven with pot holders. Place them on cookie racks to cool or let them cool on their cookie sheet.

Lollipop Cookies

Crunchy, peanutty cookies that you can make plain or as lollipops!

Here's what you need

1 cup butter
2 eggs
1 cup and 1 tablespoon dark
  brown sugar
3 teaspoons vanilla extract
½ teaspoon baking soda
1 teaspoon salt
3 cups flour
2½ cups salted peanuts
    (Spanish peanuts with skins
    on are best)

Tools

Measuring spoons
Measuring cups
Pot holders
Cookie sheet
Mixing bowls
Cooking spoon
Cooling rack
Plain wooden
  freezer sticks or
  tongue
  depressors
Flour sifter

Here's what you do

1 Measure butter, vanilla extract and sugar. Be sure to press sugar down into cup to make it tightly packed. Dump all ingredients into mixing bowl.

2 Mix well until smooth.

3 Measure flour, baking soda, and salt into sifter. Sift over butter mixture. Mix well.

4 Measure and add peanuts to dough. Mix thoroughly to get nuts all through dough.

5 Chill dough for an hour or until it is firm enough to shape.

6 Clean up the kitchen while you are waiting. Then set oven to 375 degrees.

7 Grease cookie sheet with butter. Take out chilled dough and left over sugar. Or if you prefer, use white sugar this time.

8 Take teaspoonfuls of dough as soon as it can be handled and roll into balls. You can make cookies larger if you like. Roll dough balls in sugar.

9 Place on cookie sheet about 2 inches apart. Flatten a bit and press freezer sticks into center of cookies. You don't have to make them all lollipops. You can make much larger cookies for lollipops. Just flatten them out so the center dough cooks evenly.

10 Using pot holders and adult assistance, bake in oven about 10 minutes until golden brown.

11 Remove from oven with pot holders and adult aid. Let cool on cookie rack.

Sour Cream Drop Cookies

Here are rich and dreamy cookies with a special flavor all their own. The secret is in the sour cream. Everyone will love these.

Here's what you need

¾ cup butter
2 eggs
1½ cups
    granulated
    sugar
2½ cups flour
½ teaspoon
    baking soda
Pinch of salt
⅓ cup sour cream

Tools

Measuring spoons
Measuring cups
Cooking spoon
Mixing bowl
Cup
Flour sifter
Cookie sheet
Pot holders
Wax paper

Here's what you do

1   Measure butter and sugar and place in mixing bowl. Cream them by pressing sugar into the butter with the back of your spoon. The butter will stick at first. Keep pushing and mixing until you form a smooth paste.

2　Crack open two eggs into a cup. Beat well. Add to the creamed butter in the mixing bowl. Mix thoroughly.

3　Turn on oven to 350 degrees.

4　Measure flour, salt and baking soda into the sifter. Sift over wax paper. Measure sour cream.

5　Stir some flour mixture into the mixing bowl with the creamed butter and eggs. Add some sour cream and mix. Continue adding flour and mixing and then adding sour cream and mixing until all ingredients are mixed in the bowl.

6　Grease your cookie sheet with butter. Take a teaspoonful of cookie batter and drop onto the sheet. Continue until sheet is filled. Leave some room for cookies to expand.

7　Bake in the oven for 10 minutes. Use pot holders and assistance of your adult helper. Cookies should be crisp and sandy colored.

Helpful hint

This recipe makes almost 6 dozen cookies so be sure to have extra cookie sheets on hand.

Old Fashioned Sugar Crisp Cookies

These old time cookies can be made crisp and crunchy, or softer but still crunchy. Just vary the thickness from one batch to the next.

Here's what you need

- ⅔ cup softened butter
- 2 eggs
- 2 teaspoons vanilla extract
- 4 tablespoons milk
- 4 cups flour
- 2½ teaspoons baking powder
- ½ teaspoon salt
- 1½ cups sugar

Tools

Large mixing bowl
Small bowl
Measuring cups
Measuring spoons
Rolling pin
Pastry board or pastry cloth
Cookie sheets
Wax paper
Cooking spoon
Ruler
Optional cookie cutters
Greased drinking glass
Wire Rack

Here's what you do

1 Take out butter and let it get very soft while you gather all the tools and ingredients. Measure soft butter in measuring cup and dump in large bowl.

2 Add the 2 eggs, 2 teaspoons of vanilla extract and the 4 tablespoons milk. Mash it all together with a cooking spoon until it becomes a smooth paste.

3 In the smaller bowl combine the 4 cups of flour, the 2½ teaspoons of baking powder, the ½ teaspoon of salt, and the 1½ cups of sugar. Mix well with a dry spoon.

4 Add about a third cup of the flour mixture to the big bowl with the eggs and butter. Mix well. Keep adding more flour and mixing well. When all the flour is added to the butter mixture, stir until well blended. Refrigerate dough for at least two hours, preferably overnight. Cover your bowl with wax paper.

5 Place about one quarter of the dough on pastry board or pastry cloth that has had flour thrown over it. Put the rest of the dough in the refrigerator. Coat rolling pin with flour and roll out dough on board or cloth. Set oven to 400 degrees.

6 For crispy cookies, roll out dough as thin as paper and cut cookies out with cookie cutters. For softer cookies, roll out dough to about ¼ inch thickness. Measure with ruler. Cut out with cutter or greased drinking glass rim.

7 Place cookies with spatula on lightly greased cookie sheet and bake ten minutes or until edges are brown. Check oven after five minutes to see how cookies are doing. Set to cool on wire rack.

These cookies store best in lightly fitted jars or containers. For variations you can dust the cookies with granulated sugar, sesame seeds, flavored sprinkles, or finely crushed nuts before you bake them.

Helpful hint

Always check your cookies about half way through the baking time. Cookies burn easily and ovens don't always heat evenly. Use a pot holder to open oven door. If cookies are browning unevenly, switch them around by removing the sheet from the oven and putting it back in the other side around. Close oven door tightly.

Here are some tips for mixing cookie dough. Flour should be mixed or folded in to a wet mixture with a cooking spoon or better yet a spatula. Rubber spatulas seem easier to use to me. Experiment and see what tool you like best. Never mix in flour with an electric mixer-- never use an electric mixer on anything without the aid of your adult assistant--and don't over mix the dough. If you play with any cookie dough too much, the ingredients will be TOO blended and the cookies will not be as light and flaky.

Too soft dough means too much liquid or butter has been used--refrigerate for an hour or add a tablespoon of flour.

———————— •◆• ————————

Cookie dough should always be put on COOL pans and sheets. Warm sheets will make the dough run. Let recently used sheets cool before using, or run them under cool water and dry before using on your next batch of cookies. But don't clean them with soap at this time.

Christmas Butter Cookies

These are crisp cookies you can shape by hand or with cookie cutters into Christmas shapes like stars, stockings, Santas, and Christmas trees. Or make them round. They're just as tasty.

Here's what you need

½ cup softened butter
   or margarine
½ cup powdered
   (confectioner's) sugar
½ teaspoon vanilla
   extract
1¼ cups instant, all
   purpose
   (granulated) flour
¼ teaspoon salt

Tools

Measuring cups
Measuring spoons
1 Large mixing bowl
1 Small mixing bowl
Large mixing spoon
   (wooden is best)
"Three cup" sifter
1 or 2 cookie sheets
1 Plate

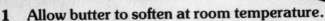

Here's what you do

1   Allow butter to soften at room temperature.

2   Put softened butter in the large mixing bowl.

3   Measure the ½ teaspoon of vanilla extract and pour it over the butter. Push it into the butter with the back of the mixing spoon.

4   Measure ½ cup of powdered sugar into a sifter. Sift the sugar over the butter into the mixing bowl.

5   Use the back of the mixing spoon to push the sugar into the butter until it forms a smooth paste. It will stick to the spoon at first. Keep mushing it and it will blend together. When blended, set aside.

6   Place measured flour and salt in the sifter. Sift the flour and salt into an empty, small mixing bowl.

7   Take about half the sifted flour and salt and add it to the large bowl with the sugar-butter paste. Mash the flour and butter mixtures together as best you can with a mixing spoon. It will be hard to mix. Pour in the rest of the flour and salt. Mix together with the spoon as best you can. Make sure you washed your hands and dried them. Then finish mixing the dough with your hands.

8   Put a plate over the bowl with the mixed dough and put the bowl in the refrigerator. Let it chill for one hour. Clean up the dishes and the kitchen while the dough chills.

9   Set the oven to 375 degrees.

10   Take an ungreased cookie sheet. Take a handful of dough and squeeze it to make it warmer. Now you can flatten it out on the cookie sheet in the shape of your choice. Push and pinch the dough to the shapes you choose. On following pages are outlines that you can trace and use as guides. Or use cookie cutters.

11   You can vary the sizes of the cookies but keep the thickness the same for all of them so they will bake evenly. When the sheet is filled with dough, put it in the hot oven and bake for about 8 minutes until the edges brown.

12   Then take out your cookies holding the sheet with pot holders and remove them from the sheet with a spatula. Place them to cool on wire racks or brown paper. Don't stack them.

These yummy cookies will crumble easily so store them in a cookie jar carefully. For variety, you can put nuts or raisins in the center of the cookies before you bake them.

Helpful hint

Always make sure to leave extra room between uncooked cookies on the baking sheet because they will grow in the oven as they bake.

Honey Christmas Kisses

Here are unusual cookies that you can decorate. But their secret greatness is their unique, sweet flavor. Save some kisses for Santa.

Here's what you need

1 cup butter
2 cups sugar
¼ cup sweet cream (light)
2 cups honey
2 tablespoons cinnamon
1 tablespoon ginger (use half as much if you use powder)
1 teaspoon powdered cloves
½ teaspoon nutmeg
Grated rind of lemon (optional)
7 cups flour

Tools

Measuring spoons
Measuring cups
Cup
Pot holders
Flour sifter
Rolling pin and pastry board
Assorted cookie cutters
Cookie sheet
Cookie rack
(optional: pencil, paper and cookie patterns from this book)
Mixing bowl
Wax paper

Here's what you do

1   Measure butter and sugar into mixing bowl. Cream together by pushing sugar into butter. Push and mix until a smooth paste is formed.

2   Measure cream and pour into bowl. Measure honey and pour into bowl. Measure spices and put into cup. Have your adult assistant help you grate the rind of a lemon into the cup. This is optional. Pour the spices into the mixing bowl.

3   Beat the mixture well.

4   Sift flour over wax paper.

5   Add sifted flour a little at a time and keep beating with spoon or fork. The dough should be stiff. If necessary you may need to add up to one cup of extra flour.

6   Roll out dough on pastry board that has had some flour spread on it. Put some flour on the rolling pin to keep dough from sticking. Roll until the dough is paper thin.

7   Turn the oven to 350 degrees.

8   Cut cookies into shapes using cookie cutters or knife and cookie patterns you have traced from this book and cut out in paper or wax paper.

9   Grease cookie sheet and then flour it lightly. Put cut cookies on sheet. Using pot holders and the aid of your adult assistant, place sheet in oven.

10   Cook for 10 to 12 minutes until cookies are light brown but not dark around the edges.

11   Remove from oven with pot holders and aid of an adult assistant. Slide cookies onto cooling rack.

12   When cool, you can decorate these cookies with one of the icings to be found in the decorator cookies section.

In Poland these cookies are used to decorate the Christmas tree. We think they taste too good to hang.

COOKIE
KITCHEN ADVISOR

Here are some tips on handling nuts and fruits. Dried fruits like raisins and apricots should be plump and moist. Sticky dried fruits like dates and figs are best chopped or sliced when very cold.

Nuts can be found in the grocery packaged in all sizes and forms. They come whole, ground, slivered, chopped, salted and so on. Chopped or slivered, unsalted nuts are the best and easiest to use. But experiment.

To keep chopped nuts and fruits from sinking to the bottom of a cookie mixture, especially in bar cookies made in a pan, coat them VERY lightly with a bit of flour before sprinkling them on the dough.

Christmas Decorator Cookies

Here's a special section to show you how to make all kinds of decorator cookies and sculptures. Here are tasty cookies--buttery and gingerbready--and a baker's clay you don't eat at all. But it will make decorations that will keep until next Christmas. Look for the special cookie patterns in this book. And here are three different and delicious cookie frostings and glazes which you can color your cookies with.

Decorator cookies are great Christmas tree decorations, Put them on special presents, in your window, or on your door. You can even make cookie Christmas cards!

No. 1

Here's a recipe to
decorate your tree with,
or your presents, or
just to eat. And you
can make these cookies
into anything you like--
reindeer, stockings,
Santa, stars, Christmas
trees--you name it.

Here's what you need

For the cookies--
⅔ cup butter
1 cup granulated sugar
1 egg
¾ teaspoon vanilla extract
2¼ cups flour
¾ teaspoon baking powder
    (double-acting)
¼ teaspoon salt
½ teaspoon nutmeg

For frosting--
1 cup POWDERED sugar
2 tablespoons milk
Food colors...red, green, and
    and other colors
Various candy decorations:
    silver dots, sugar sparkles,
    sprinkles of chocolate, gum
    drops, raisins too.

Tools

Measuring spoons
Measuring cups
Cooking spoon
Large mixing bowl
Cup
Flour sifter
Large plate
Wax paper
Pencil
Scissors
Plain paper
Cookie sheet
Rolling pin
Table knife
Wire rack
Pastry board or
    pastry cloth or
    cutting board
Small mixing bowl
Colored string
    or yarn

Here's what you do

1 Measure butter and sugar and put in large bowl. Cream together by pushing sugar into butter with back of spoon. Keep pushing and mixing until a smooth paste is made.

2 Break the egg into a cup. Be sure to remove any egg shell from the cup. Pour egg into creamed butter and sugar.

3 Pour measured vanilla extract on top of mixture in bowl. Beat quickly with spoon (or fork) until the mixture turns into a smooth yellow batter. Set mixing bowl aside.

4 Measure flour, baking powder, salt and nutmeg into sifter. Sift over wax paper.

5 Pour about half the sifted flour mixture into the bowl of batter stir slowly with spoon until flour is well blended.

6 Add the rest of the flour. Mix with spoon. Mix with your CLEAN hands. Mix until the dough is stiff.

7 Push dough down tightly into bottom of bowl Cover with plate. Store in refrigerator for two hours.

8 While dough is cooling in the refrigerator, clean up the kitchen and wash the dishes.

9 Now the decorator fun. Get some plain paper, wax paper, or tracing paper. Trace some of the patterns you will find in this book. Or make up your own cookie shapes. They should be about 3 or 4 inches long.

10   Cut out the shapes. Then set the oven to 400 degrees.

11   Get the cookie sheet. Don't bother greasing it. Get the rolling pin and table knife ready.

12   Take out the dough from the refrigerator. It will be very hard. Use the knife to poke the dough away from the bowl. Turn the bowl upside down on the cookie sheet. The dough will fall out.

13   Spread the dough with your hands. Pat it and push it down. Push together all the crumbs that fall off. Either in the cookie sheet, or on a board, flatten the dough into a pancake about 9 inches by 12 inches and about 1 inch thick.

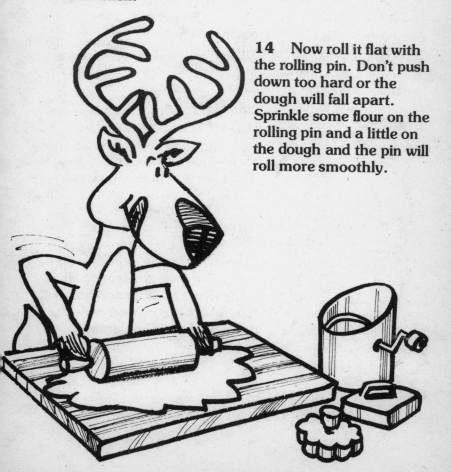

14   Now roll it flat with the rolling pin. Don't push down too hard or the dough will fall apart. Sprinkle some flour on the rolling pin and a little on the dough and the pin will roll more smoothly.

15 With the flat dough on the cookie sheet roll it a few last times to make it all even in height. It will be smooth in the middle with no bumps. The edges will be crumbly.

16 Put the cookie sheet in the oven with pot holders and the aid of your adult assistant. Let it stay in for about 8 minutes. The dough will be brown at the edges.

17 Take out the sheet with pot holders and let cool on a rack for about 15 minutes.

18 Place your cookie patterns around the cookie sheet as closely together as possible. You should be able to make about 9 big cookies. Cut them out with the knife using the patterns as your guide. Don't separate them. Just cut. Put a toothpick through the top of each cookie you want to hang on your tree or presents. Let them cool completely before you separate them.

19 While cookies are cooling, make your own frosting.

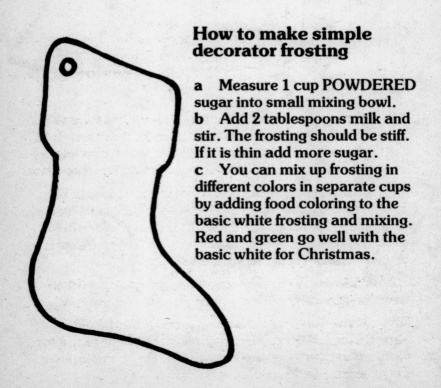

How to make simple decorator frosting

a Measure 1 cup POWDERED sugar into small mixing bowl.
b Add 2 tablespoons milk and stir. The frosting should be stiff. If it is thin add more sugar.
c You can mix up frosting in different colors in separate cups by adding food coloring to the basic white frosting and mixing. Red and green go well with the basic white for Christmas.

20 When your cookies are cool--about the time you
have finished making frosting--separate them carefully.
Put all the cookies on one plate. Put the left over pieces
of cookie from in between your cut-outs on another plate.

21 Frost and decorate the cookies any way you like.
In colors and in basic white. With sprinkles and raisins
for eyes if you make animal or Santa cookies. Gum
drops will be nice in the frosting too. When one side is
dry, you can work on the other side.

22 While working you may want to snack on the in-
between pieces. Very tasty. You can frost them too.

23 When finished decorating, string the thread or
yarn through the cookies that have the holes in the top.
You are ready to decorate your tree. Or your windows.
Or presents. Or just go ahead and eat' em.

Christmas Decorator Cookies No. 2

Dark Dough Ginger Cookies

This is a professional recipe for cookies that will hold their shape and flavor a long time. They look great when decorated with colored icings and glazes because they are so dark. Ginger delicious.

Here's what you need

½ cup butter
½ cup dark brown sugar
½ cup molasses
3½ cups flour
½ teaspoon salt
1 teaspoon baking soda
1 teaspoon ginger
2 teaspoons cinnamon
½ cup buttermilk
½ teaspoon vinegar

Tools

Cookie sheet
Measuring spoons
Measuring cups
Pot holders
Pencil, paper, scissors or cookie cutters
Rolling pin and pastry board
Cooling rack
Table knife
Mixing bowls
Flour sifter

Here's what you do

1 Measure butter, sugar, and molasses into mixing bowl. Cream together by pressing sugar into the butter with the back of a spoon. Keep pushing and mixing until a smooth paste is made.

2 Measure buttermilk and vinegar. Measure flour, salt, baking soda, and spices into sifter. Sift over empty mixing bowl. Add some of the flour mixture to the creamed butter and mix.

3 Add some of the buttermilk and vinegar to the creamed mixture and mix. Continue adding flour mixture and then buttermilk and vinegar and mixing. When all ingredients are in one bowl and well mixed, chill in refrigerator at least one hour.

4 Turn on oven to 350 degrees.

5 Trace cookie patterns from this book on wax paper or plain paper. Make up your own patterns, too. Cut out patterns.

6 When dough is chilled, remove from refrigerator. Flour pastry board and rolling pin. Roll out cold dough until it is about ¼ inch thick. Lay patterns on dough and cut them out. Or use cookie cutters.

7 Lightly grease cookie sheet. Lift patterned cookie dough carefully with your clean hands and place on cookie sheet.

8 Using pot holders and the assistance of your adult helper, place cookies in oven and bake 10 to 15 minutes.

9 Remove from oven with pot holder and place on cooling rack.

10 When cookies are still warm but not hot, you can decorate them with any of the icings and glazes presented in this section.

Here are some basic tips for decorating cookies. Crisp thin cookies are generally best for decorating. But recipes have been provided in this book for special decorating projects.

Decorating can be done before baking with colored sugars, caramel or chocolate chips, jimmies and candy balls, and other goodies you will find in the baking section of your grocery.

After baking, plain cookies that have been cooled can be decorated with icing and then covered with colored sprinkles or sugar. To Ice Nice--drop a teaspoonful of icing on the center of each cookie. Spread it with a small spatula or butter knife in strokes that move around in circles.

No. 3
Don't Eat Me Dough

Sometimes known as Baker's Clay, this recipe is for decorations you design and color for your tree. BUT YOU DON'T EAT THEM. They last indefinitely. Great for windows, trees, presents, special Christmas Cards, and...well just use your imagination. Good to make sculpture and clay figures too.

Here's what you need

1 cup salt
3 to 4 cups flour
1¼ to 1½ cups water
Food coloring, or
    plastic model paint
Bit of butter

Tools

Measuring cups
Mixing bowl
Cookie sheet
Pot holders
Pencil
Cookie patterns made from
    this book on tracing paper
optional: cookie cutters, plate
Knife

Here's what you do

1   Measure and combine ingredients in bowl. Put flour on hands.

2   Knead dough by squeezing and mixing with your hands.

3   After five minutes, if you feel dough needs more water, add a bit very carefully. Put more flour on hands if dough sticks.

4   Grease cookie sheet with bit of butter. Turn on oven with help of your adult assistant to 275 degrees.

5   Take cookie patterns which you have traced on paper and cut out. Place dough ball about size of walnut over a pattern. Flatten out with your hand until it covers pattern.

6 Cut away excess dough from edge of pattern leaving cookie shape. Repeat with other patterns. Place finished dough patterns on cookie sheet.

7 Or use cookie cutters and press into dough on plate.

8 For hangings, press pencil through top of dough pattern to make hole where string can be threaded.

9 You can also make statues and sculptures. Just shape the dough any way you like. To build up layers, paste one piece of dough to another by coating the bottom layer with water. Water will act as glue.

10 If you like, you can mix food coloring into the dough, or run it over the finished dough pattern. Food coloring doesn't work the same on this dough as it does on eatable cookies, but it can make interesting effects. I just paint my uneatable sculptures after I bake 'em.

11 Using pot holders place your cookies and sculptures on the TOP rack of the oven. Bake for about 2 to 3 hours in a slow oven. This means low heat.

12 Take out of oven carefully with pot holders and aid of adult assistant. Let cool. The dough will be hard as a rock. If a piece falls off, it can be glued back with Elmer's Glue.

13 Decorate your cookies and sculpture with plastic model paint. Or you can use any of the decorator glazes mentioned in this section.

Remember, on this recipe - NO TASTING!

Christmas Decorator Cookies

Additional Frostings

Just in case you'd like to experiment with some different frostings for your decorator cookies--and who wouldn't since icings and frostings are some of the tastiest things you can make--here are a few great recipes.

Cream Glaze
Very rich and satisfying.

Here's what you need

2 cups <u>confectioner's</u> sugar
½ teaspoon vanilla (or almond) extract
½ cup milk or preferably heavy cream

Tools

Measuring cups
Measuring spoons
Mixing bowl
Saucepan
Table knife
Pot holder
Cooking spoon
Food Coloring
Flour sifter

Here's what you do

1   Sift sugar over wax paper. Put in mixing bowl with vanilla or almond extract.

2   Heat milk or cream in saucepan. Use low heat. Stir in sugar slowly until you have the right thickness. You want the glaze to be thick.

3   Remove from heat with potholder and pour into bowl.

4 If you wish, glaze can be divided into separate cups and a few drops of food coloring can be added to each portion.

5 Use table knife and spread on cookies to be decorated.

Always use glazes as quickly as you can. They will harden as they cool. Sprinkles or nuts can be pressed into glaze before it hardens on cookies.

Sugar Glaze
Thin, hard and sweet.

Here's what you need

1/3 cup <u>confectioner's</u> sugar
1½ tablespoons cornstarch
½ teaspoon vanilla or
    almond extract
1 to 3 tablespoons hot water

Tools

Measuring spoons
Measuring cups
Mixing bowl
Food coloring
  (optional)
Cooking spoon

Here's what you do

1 Measure and mix sugar, cornstarch, flavoring into mixing bowl.

2 Stir in hot water 1 tablespoon at a time and mix until you have a smooth paste.

3 Spread on WARM cookies with small spoon.

4 If you wish, you can separate the glaze into separate cups and mix in a few drops of food coloring into each cup.

5 If glaze cools and hardens, thin it with more hot water.

Professional Decorator Icing

Excellent for artistic coloring of patterned cookies to hang on your tree or presents.

Here's what you need

1 egg white
⅛ teaspoon cream of tartar
1⅔ cups of confectioner's sugar
Food coloring

Tools

Measuring spoons
Measuring cups
Cooking spoon
Small bowls
Cup
Knife
Flour sifter

Here's what you do

1 Crack egg open over the cup. Let white slip out but hold in the yolk. This is tricky. Let your adult assistant guide you.

2 Add a pinch of cream of tartar to egg white. This is about 1/8 teaspoon. Beat with spoon until stiff.

3 Sift sugar over wax paper. Add sugar a little at a time to egg white and beat briskly.

4 To add food coloring, separate icing into various small bowls and drop in selected colors until you have the shade you like.

5 Spread with knife on cookies.

Did you know that most cookies, baked or unbaked, keep well in the freezer? Left over cookie dough should be rolled up into a log. Wrap it in plastic or wax paper before freezing. When you want to use it, just thaw it!

Baked cookies keep best when stored in a metal or plastic box with a tight fitting top. Put the cookies in one layer. Cover with freezer wrap or wax paper. Add another layer of cookies. Cover with wrap. Keep filling the box until no more cookies will fit in. Cover the last layer with wrap and freeze.

Tools of the cookie trade

Each recipe in my cookie cookbook will tell you exactly what you will need to make that particular cookie. Here is an illustrated guide to all the tools mentioned in this book. Refer to this guide when you forget what a special tool looks like. Use the right tool for the right job and you will make better cookies.

Mixing bowls: some big, some small.

measuring spoons: sets usually include tablespoon, teaspoon, ½ & ¼ teaspoon

measuring cup

flour sifter

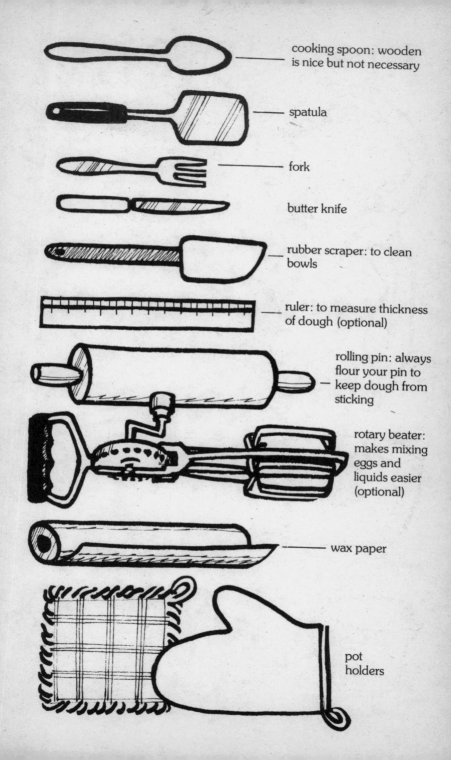

cooking spoon: wooden is nice but not necessary

spatula

fork

butter knife

rubber scraper: to clean bowls

ruler: to measure thickness of dough (optional)

rolling pin: always flour your pin to keep dough from sticking

rotary beater: makes mixing eggs and liquids easier (optional)

wax paper

pot holders

Tools of the cookie trade

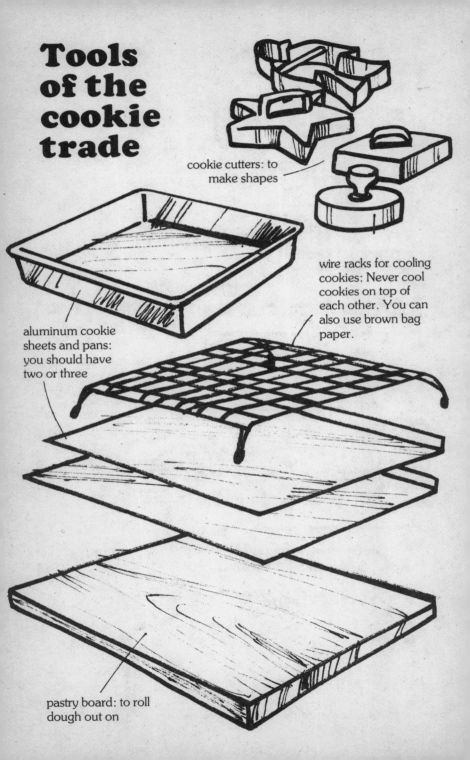

cookie cutters: to make shapes

wire racks for cooling cookies: Never cool cookies on top of each other. You can also use brown bag paper.

aluminum cookie sheets and pans: you should have two or three

pastry board: to roll dough out on